Of The First Magnitude

~I~

I0169438

~Volume 1~

Facing Revelation

An Emerging

~Volume 2~

iRise

An Algorhythm of Freedom

~Volume 3~

Quantum Engineering

Introspecting the Rabbit Hole

~Volume 4~

Algorhythmic Insight

Poetic Analysis of the Journey

Copyright Notice:

Read it!

Integrate it!

Live it!

Truth, that is...

Emergent Strategies LLC
PO Box 245
Winona, MO. 65588
https://3m3r3g.com
orders@3m3rg3.com

ISBN: 978-1-7337454-4-4

Quantity sales. Special discounts are available on quantity purchases by corporations, associations, and others. For details, contact the publisher at the address above.

Cover Art: Sam Whelan - https://www.samwhelan.net/

~ Volume 4 ~

Algorhythmic Insight

Poetic Analysis of the Journey

By Michael Phoenix

Part 1

~ a journey into light ~

Walk with me as I journey...

Where've You Gone?

You see me
In everything I do
I see you
When I choose to

I give thanks
For all your gifts
I ask for help
I get no answer

What have I done
To lose sight
Where've you gone
To hide from me

I want to see
Your beauty
But you make
Sight so difficult

I try my best to
Give what you do
Why do I feel
Like a lost soul

Sitting here
Trying to listen
I don't hear
You often enough

Do I make
It difficult to see
Am I the one
Who hides

I beg you

Please show me
Take my hand
To lead me

And I will follow!

(1/20/2006 5:52pm)

I'm Cryin

When times get rough I
Want to cry inside

I feel like breakin down
And cryin inside

Givin up feels like, fuck it
I'm cryin inside

I'm cryin Inside,
I'm cryin inside, For You

Hope runs through my veins,
Faith is my foundation

I feel your power inside
But my mind wanders

I can see your truth
It's what gets me through

Why do I feel the pains,
I can't stand my hesitation

When times get rough I
Want to cry inside

I feel like breakin down
And cryin inside

Givin up feels like, fuck it
I'm cryin inside

I'm cryin Inside,
I'm cryin inside, For You

I can see you bein abused
But you keep on givin

I want to live in your vision
I can't get over my indecision

It's so hard to find my true life
So many choices just bring strife

I'm eagerly wantin to be used
With helpin to get people livin

When times get rough I
Want to cry inside

I feel like breakin down
And cryin inside

Givin up feels like, fuck it
I'm cryin inside

I'm cryin Inside,
I'm cryin inside, For You, Jesus

(1/20/2006 6:25pm)

My God

Oh my God
You give me strength

Yes Lord
You show me the way

Jesus Christ
You've paved the path

Live with God
I live in your will

Holy Spirit
I'm feeling your power

Blessed Virgin
You're a vision of grace

Oh Mother
Father Creator
God

I give you thanks
For all you have shown

I Forgive all who have trespassed
I request forgiveness for mine

Fill me with your condition-less love
Forever will I walk in your light

(1/20/2006 6:45pm)

Love in My Life

I live with your love in my
Heart till the end of days

I can't get over the beauty
You show in all your ways

I ache when I think of
Losing you to the dark

Only in your arms
Does true love spark

(3/9/2006)

Questions for His Egoness?

What does he really want,
always lost in fascination
of the future, or pursing
the truth of the past?

When does he live in the
known of now? Will he ever
be satisfied with who he is,
or always concerned with
external wealth?

Can he clear his mind to
hear the answer that has
never been heard, but
remains to the hereafter?

The complications seem to
exponentially complicate,
caring only about curing the
curiosity of physiological
concerns.

Do his desires dare dream
about the definition of life,
or does he wish to remain
dreaming in the density of
darkness that surrounds his
every detriment to Self?

Perhaps the still small voice
will one day slice the slimy
salutations he honors in the
hedonistic.

Maybe the mind will morph
his materialistic overdoing to

the passionate pursuit of the
ever-lasting love and light.

Can he ever come to terms
with the constant conflict
contained controlling
nothing but the loss of
control?

Will he let the True-Self
actualize his being to bring
the benefit of beneficence,
and vibe the flow that
emanates from the eternal
playground of Love?

(10/22/2006 11:46pm)

Truth Transcendent

The truth transcendent...perpetually permeating eternally empowering...forever fermenting the evolution of Unconditional Love's conscious revolution.

Subjectively subject the mind to the divine object of metaphysical aetheric objectivity. Flip the perception of separation to walk the eternal fire of the soul's manifestation...love and light.

Externalize the internal...Internalize the external. Objectify the subjective...subjectify the objective. Make the fantastic the realistic, and the realistic the fantastic.

In the end of it all is the beginning of everything and nothing all the same...for in the single moment of life's linear perpetuation is the key to realizing the Self that is our infinitely spherical eternal manifestation.

Materialize the imagination...mystify the realization, for in concrete explanation is the position of a sophist's clever egoic deception.

Truth remains eternal...never afflicted by the limited awareness of the fear filled self-image of nothing more than the material. Broaden the horizon of perception and see the eternal self residing unabated in the realms of the ethereal.

The light and love bursting through the consciousness of that which is the alpha and omega is proof enough. Open the chakra of the sacred heart...balance the flame that burns with the brightness of...of your soul.

Purify the darkness of ignorance...permit the
divinity of monadic majesty...perpetuate the
dedication of Self-realization...prevent the density
of inner inconsistency...

eat the Earth...breath the Air...drink the
Water...transmute within the Fire...Become the
unification for the sake of unity. Let loose the
pride of limitation...embrace the humility of
infinity.

Living a life OF the world compounds confusion
and creates complexities of a creation that is
effectual through causality. Realize the simplicity
by living IN the world to understand that you are
the reason of the effects.

Remembrance of God's sole self salutation relies
on searching the soul for truth and divine
identification. Relinquish the conceptualization of
the incomprehensible precept known as God.

What is God other than that creation that is
speaking forth from the mental machinations
of...the source? Boundaries justify the
perpetuation of dogmatic degradation in the name
of divination.

Defining an existence that exists infinitely is a
duty of the fool. In the definition is the limitation
of static stagnation. Open the mind not to the
concepts of self-contraception, but to the
realization that breeds infinite fertility; ever
growing, ever changing, ever initiating forward
from agreed self-limitation to the unfathomable
independent unification of the collective co-
creation called God.

Feel the truth, speak the truth, hear the truth, see the truth, be the truth, know the truth...Act according to the truth brought forth by the Unconditional Love of all that is, was, and shall be,

Denounce deception...indoctrinate innocence...bestow benevolence...purify pride...catalyze congruence...adulate absolution...

Feed not on the fear of apathy, move within the motivation of the majestic almighty. Sit, Relax...Breathe, Relax...Soak in the love...Illuminate with the light... now extend and revolutionize the evolution of your lovingly Unconditional consciousness.

(12/23/2006 9:12pm)

WAKEing UP

In the waking of my psyche,
within the drama of mankind's epic tragedy;
my soul has lead me to see
that our current philosophy
of military and Industrial promiscuity
has caused a global lobotomy of our ethical cortex
and moral motor skills.

In retrospect,
the halls of history have led me to see
that the mission of the leaders elect
with their "war on terrorism"
was brought about
by our abject ignorance
while we claim innocence
from a stance of indifference
brought about by our
cowardly unwillingness
to stand up
for the principle of
benevolent beneficence.

But with the waning of my egoic intellect
and releasing the need to logically circumspect;
it has caused my mind to recollect
what truly is;
that is the marvelous magnificence
of our angelic embodiment.
But with the current mode of neglect
towards the power to interconnect
and focus our consciousness
toward the betterment of social interdependence;
it has become glaringly apparent
that the obvious question is,
where the hell is our leadership
that is 'of, by, and for the people'...

well... people?

We claim that our land
is the shining beacon of democracy.
How can that be when our ability
to question idiocy
is met with administrative scrutiny
that attempts to portray the lunacy
of a multi-million dollar
spoon-fed commissioned conspiracy
is the truth to justify
a multi-trillion dollar corporate sponsored heresy;
heresy as it pertains to the legality
of mass murder in the name
of peace and harmony?

The time for questioning
the validity of spirituality
is over.

Lay aside the dogmatic skepticism
of indoctrinated mechanical materialism
to introspect and learn the dialect
flowing in harmonious vibration.

Develop the accuracy
of the mental and emotional faculties
to direct the intent
of the soul's gravitational law
so as to attract the abundance
of universal exuberance.

Disconnect the disrespect
that flows from egoic malcontent.
Inject the select aspect
of the soul's idiolect
to connect to the highest respect
so as to project the will

of the grand architect that inhabits every aspect
of our spiritual inheritance.

Only then will we truly come to understand
that our transcendence of global destruction and violence
depends on our social interdependence
that emanates and flows forth from our undeniable
spiritual interconnectedness – Love!

So in the words of Mr. Robert Nesta Marley,
"Now that you've seen the light,
Stand Up for Your Right!"

(12/28/2006 2:05 am)

YOU ARE LOST!

Feeling lost when
Looking in the mirror
to see the illusion of
the perpetuated identification
that I call "me,"
I find a spark of the
greater one
waiting to return me into infinity.

Believing for a moment
that "I" am simply all that
I see,
I look to the left
and then to the right
and I begin
to remember
that "I" am much more
than this fleshy identity that
I call Mike.

In that space of
my spiraling harmonious
evolution where I see
a greater depth in
this blade of grass
that exists to shine its
brilliance and jump start
my heart to flow in the
river of love
that brings through torrents
of my golden pranic inheritance.

No longer lost in the
perpetuation of limited
identification, but rather,
standing in the bliss

of heavenly grace,
shining as a beacon,
choosing to remain,
living to remember,
loving all the way,
I AM who I AM

(5/18/2007 9:19pm)

You are THE Light!!!

"i'm honored that you say that
because it is what I have
dedicated my life to…
to be that beacon,
calling everyone home
and now you have seen
it and answered,
in that answer is your beacon
to call to others as I have
called to you.
and together we shall all
shine the brilliance that we truly are
uniting humanity
in the love and light of
our divine self.
it is a partnership,
a co-creation,
the yin-yang of life
and together we
walk the razor's edge
to manifest this
as a beacon for all humanity
inspiring them to loving action
calling them to embrace
their love and their light
calling them home
to the place we have forgotten
to the place that resides in our hearts
to the place we truly long to be
TOGETHER"

(5/19/2007 10:55am)

Journey Into
Illumination

Creating the waves
that ripple into the
breath of eternity...

Breathing the light
that illuminates the
void of creation...

Spiraling inward to
see the infinite golden
presence that is who I AM...

Evolving beyond
boundaries to
become the
benevolent beacon of
a bodhisattva...

Vibrating the
universality of a
vivacious Love that is
all that *is*...

Manifesting the will of
the One who is,
who is to come
and who has
been...

Propagating the
peace that presents
the presence of
omnipotence...

Bring forth that which
is the truth of the
eternal Self to sanctify
the sacred essence of
our divinity!!!

(6/4/2007 6:54pm)

BE…Simply Be

The endless beauty flows on
The valleys of flowers
The limitless sky above
The caress of the wind across my cheek
The rolling tenderness as the wind glides across the land

Swimming in the infinite bliss
of love's ever-present ocean.

The sight of creation
Creating the sight
That creates creation

~OPEN~
~OPEN~
~OPEN~

Sweet child of Love

OPEN
OPEN
OPEN

to the tenderness – magnifying, multiplying, radiating,
illuminating the sacred divinity of love

~OPEN~
~OPEN~
~OPEN~

Shower me with the golden rain of who I AM

Breeeeaaaathhhhe

Soak into the consciousness of the present

Breeeeaaaathhhhe

Surrender to the willingness of the eternal expansion into the
ever-present presence of THIS eternal moment

Smile – intensify the delight
Laugh – multiply the bliss

Surrender into ecstasy – Forgive THE illusion:
What illusion? "my" illusion!

Exist nowhere – Exist here...
Exist then – Exist now...
Exist never – Exist forever...

EXIST for the sake of existing – Do not confine the
necessity – EXIST

For what is the necessity
of that which is not necessary?
EXIST

Illuminate imagination
EXIST

Dive into possibility
EXIST

Shed the suffering...
Release the confusion...
Let go of the guilt...

OPEN to the existence
of our eternally existing
spiritual existence...*EXIST*

Connect the cord...
Fire YOUR grid,

And THE grid will be fired

EXIST

Radiate the chakras…
Spin the crystals…
Let the flowers bloom…

OPEN

For openness
For Existence

OPEN and EXIST

I AM

(7/16/2007 4:17am)

Your Paradise

"Paint the rainbow of your paradise,"
Tis the secret the heart shared with the mind.

"Paint the rainbow of your paradise,
Don't you know it's your world," she continued.

"Paint the rainbow of your paradise,
It can be anything you want it to be."

"Paint the rainbow of your paradise,
What you see NOW is your creation."

"Did you know the sun never stops shining? Paint the
rainbow of your paradise," she went on.

"All that you think you know and perceive is how you paint
the rainbow of your paradise."

"I'll tell you another secret," she said.
"Open me up, for I am the brush that colors the rainbow of
your paradise."

(7/30/2007 3:55am)

Raw Transparency of My Mind

Come listen to my realest rawest emotions, thoughts &
feelins ever put in black and white, Unedited, unmodified,
untainted & unadulterated,

Livin in a world where the present world-wide illusion OF
pain, sufferin and misery exist as misting the night, &

My brothers and sisters runnin around cryin and screamin
and fightin worried about the image and the comfort
depressed & stressed, traumatized by the presence of evil
within them

I sit back watchin the grand projection of our hellish
hallucination. Sometimes cryin, sometimes laughin,
sometimes just sittin by & anticipatin the realization of a
higher revelation...Sympathizin with the misery, knowin we
created ever evil emission

But then again all the darkness has the
counterpart of its glorious illumination.

Honesty sets the individual free is what I heard from the
Masters of the illumination,
How can I be fully honest when it seems
I'm the only one willin to stand for the mission?

Stayin true for the sanctity of life's purest
poetic creative infusion of a higher unified inclusion.
Blissing in the experience of the purity of God's greatest
illuminated b-l-esson

Bless On with humility is said to be a path
to the highest heights of Unconditional Love. How can I
live with humility when it sometimes seems I'm the only
one willin to be a selfless warrior especially with a witness
and testimony of this humiliation we call a nation?

It only takes one to pave the path of highest vibration,
carryin the creation of ripples into eternal salvation. Blissin
in the experience of the purity of God's
greatest illuminated b-l-esson

In the words of the realest rappa ever livin
Tupac told me the other day he's reached eternity "In this
game the lesson's in your eyes to see Though things
change, the future's still inside of me We must remember
that tomorrow comes after the dark So you will always be in
my heart, with unconditional love."

Honestly I sometimes question the mission of the highest
interest, that is experiencing the realization of eternal
illumination flowing & vibrating forth from the source of the
deepest river in creation

And to keep the rawness of transparency, I
sometimes think it's all for nothin; standin, screamin,
shoutin, from the
heights of my egoic intellect I sometimes
forget that on the path of enlightenment
my biggest obstacle is the devils and demons that exist
inside of me as egocentricity.

Witnessing the duality of the darkest evil I ever witnessed
exist inside of me, it has me look on the world with
sympathy and extend my compassion, knowin we're
witnessing the expression of the devil that exists inside of
everybody.

Sometimes it appears to me as pathetic
that we still got people who walk around apathetic to the
perverse injustice & indifference perpetrated on my
brothers & sisters by the choice of our collectivity
to judge and separate the perception of individuality as
more important than the extension of our inner unity.

In the times that seem to test my commitment, I find myself
cryin and wishin we'd all just wake up from the insanity of
this global stick up, giving away our rights to live a life of
fear that we never
even created with our own freed imagination

Instead we got a spoon fed indoctrination of separation
perpetuated by our unwillingness to look beyond
the perception of the appearances.

The Legend said it straight sayin "None but ourselves can
free our minds." I take solace knowin that I'm not here to
be a leader, just make the change by livin according to the
eternal principle of bein the change that I seek.

So long I sat in the well of misery wishing I could blow up
the world, takin all the tragedy and suffering with me.

Now on the other side of a bridge built by a brilliant
rainbow emanating from within the heart of our unity it
appears to me that we already exist within our infinity.

Eternity is said to be the treasure of entering the infinite
sea, takin time to witness the deflection we unconsciously
agree to moment after moment, I can't help but think I'm
crazy, I have no identity in this infinite unity.

Am I the only one that sees what I see? Do you see the
reality of a destiny already written – we're already
enlightened, we just have to accept it, and forgive the idea
of our forgetfulness to experience the bliss emanatin form
within the heart of our unity, it appears to me that we already
exist within our infinity.

Perhaps it's just a fantasy. Then I remember that its more
real to me than the pain I used to call reality.

Happiness is a goal that's already been givin to us, we just
have to open our hearts to its freest expression, & sit back
blissin in the purity of God's greatest illuminated
b-l-esson...
Unconditional Love

(10/31/2007 11:14pm)

We, the Warriors of Peace, do declare...

It's a shame they spit this venom upon us... "We need your freedoms for security of my idea of national imperial interests." Political & Religious doctrines of duality and disparity... They must not've herd the news.

It's a revolution...Freedom

It's a revolution...Light

It's a revolution...Love

This is the people's champion...the people who are destined to be free...Freedom...This is the people's champion...the people who know the Reality of... limitless love your neighbor as you are the one in unlimited unity...Source your Self...Love...This is the people's champion...the people who espouse the colors of every sort of individuality in the enlightened unity of light.

It's a revolution...Freedom

It's a revolution...Light

It's a revolution...Love

Yo, WE are the Warriors of Peace

(11/5/2007 10:53pm)

I & I

I – Burning in the consciousness
of man do I shine

I – Born not of the flesh yet in the
flesh do I possess

I – Flashing with waves of
cataclysms do I create

I – Formless and boundless beyond
the measures I live

I – Freely loving, forever
pulsating do I radiate

I – Purely crystal, shining
infinity I cannot escape

Ally is Freedom to I

Sword is Light to I

Armor is Love to I

Peace is Mission to I

I – Flowing in torrents of
heaven's gold is I

I – Built solid on Zion's
Mountain is I

I – Calm with Breath's sacred
pulse is I

I – Forever illuminating cycles
of dark is I

I – Claiming power with Lion's
roar is I

I – Piercing illusion does in-sight
produce is I

I – Iron is fortitude in depths of
truth is I

Ally is Freedom to I

Sword is Light to I

Armor is Love to I

Peace is Mission to I

I & I
Source and center of
Unconditional Love

(11/18/2007 11:05pm)

Hahaha...It's a Game

Reach into the depths of serenity,
Live a life of sanctified solitude
Bless On with abundance selflessly
Servin in the light of Jah's highest height

Whoa to men of false understandin
Check the source of perpetuated indifference, Yep
Apathy, serves the path of passionless indecision to
Separation and guilty systems of death and,
Destruction no longer serves the moral fiber
Struck in the mind of man's highest pursuit to,
Truth is a source found by the inwardly seeking to
Illuminate the illusions of darkness,
It's a simple process to the Mountain,
Come off the pulpit of systematic indoctrination,
The false justice of self-glorification,
Permeating the darkness in dishonesty

Hahaha

Reach into the depths of serenity,
Live a life of sanctified solitude
Bless On with abundance selflessly
Servin in the light of Jah's highest height

It's a cycle ya see, the repetition of history,
Democratic fascism, our despots best friend.
Legalize the usurpation of freedom and rights in the
name of thwarting the terror of a nation, Yep,
It's actually kinda funny, to see the few tryin
to belittle the spirit of the many.
It's a cycle ya see, the repetition of history,
Influx of spirit comes, infuses the actions of man,
Risin Up, Rebelling, Revolutionizing the system, Yep,
Always comin back to the freedom of birth right
creation.

Hahaha

Reach into the depths of serenity,
Live a life of sanctified solitude
Bless On with abundance selflessly
Servin in the light of Jah's highest height

In the heights of light it's seen that it'll never happen,
The oppression of Jah's greatest gift, the very
presence of the Lion's essence coursing our veins is
Jah's present,
The downtrodden will always seek to rise in
evolution, Yep, its called natural selection, the spirit
of man is the strength that sees us through the battle,
we've seen it through dismantling systematic chattel,
Slavery is an old game played by a fool tryin to
donwpress the source of infinite significance, Love,
it's a path of more courage that'll never lead you to
insignificance,

Hahaha

Reach into the depths of serenity,
Live a life of sanctified solitude
Bless On with abundance selflessly
Servin in the light of Jah's highest height

You see, those who promote the philosophy of
military and industrial promiscuity in place of the
honor available in the selfless servitude of
Unconditional Love believe in a world where we exist
as pawns worthy of sacrifice. Before you know it,
your ass winds up in a contradiction, where you think
your freedom is protected by the offense of
innocence in the name of weapons of mass
destruction...hahaha, you've been foiled, it's all for
the oil, the monster of industry must be fed, and now

you're here to serve the nation's best interest, the
death and destruction of human innocence we call
terrorists.

Hahaha

Reach into the depths of serenity,
Live a life of sanctified solitude
Bless On with abundance selflessly
Servin in the light of Jah's highest height

The Legend said it, those who serve the false pretense
are the big fish that seek to eat the little with guiltiness
always resting on their conscience.
The halls of history
have seen it before me, we shall know the works of
our fathers by the presence of the life we're given, it's
a choice, we can sit in a-pathetic indifference or cycle
through the depths of conscious thought to see the
fundamental truth that WE ARE.

Hahaha

Reach into the depths of serenity,
Live a life of sanctified solitude
Bless On with abundance selflessly
Servin in the light of Jah's highest height

Rising to the height of light may seem like a fool's
plight, shit, look what we did to our brother Jesus.
Teachin a path of forgiveness and appreciation for
the presence of our neighbors, we take him and
slaughter him to keep the comfort and safety of the
system. Yeah, don't forget about our brother, the man
who freed a nation through civil disobedience,
gonedy, adios, see ya later, bye bye he said to the
imperialists. Who thought he'd inspire a King to rise

to the heights walkin the journey by bein a pacifist.
ASSASINATED

Hahaha

Reach into the depths of serenity,
Live a life of sanctified solitude
Bless On with abundance selflessly
Servin in the light of Jah's highest height

Don't fret, they live on in consciousness, the light,
cuz that's the truth they came to shed, we are the
ones to see the truth by being our vision that takes us
to the change we envision. It's our imagination
through action that creates the ripples echoing
through the ocean of eternity. Embrace the love
showered by Jah's maternity, It's our mother united as
one with our father embedded in the soul created in
the image with a likeness equal to the omnipotence.

Hahaha

Reach into the depths of serenity,
Live a life of sanctified solitude
Bless On with abundance selflessly
Servin in the light of Jah's highest height

Hahaha

It's a game

Hahaha

It's a game

Hahaha

Wake from the illusion

It's a game

Hahahahahahahahahahahahahaha

(11/19/2007 3:16pm)

Lightworker's Manifesto

We are Lightworkers
Dedicated to the highest truth
Committed to the broadest love
Devoted to the deepest faith
Extending to the furthest sight

We are Lightworkers,
No longer do we allow the
Knife of judgement to separate,
Allowing fear and illusion to
Control our lives.

We, the workers of light declare
Unconditional Love as our
Reality through expression.

We, the workers of light
Are the illumination of unity
In the night of duality.

We are Lightworkers
Dedicated to the highest truth
Committed to the broadest love
Devoted to the deepest faith
Extending to the furthest sight

We are Lightworkers,
Holding the breath of compassion
For all, selflessly serving in humility
The Will of the Most High.

We, the workers of light declare
Oneness as our reality
In creation.

We, the workers of light

Are the illumination of unity
In the night of duality

We are Lightworkers
Dedicated to the highest truth
Committed to the broadest love
Devoted to the deepest faith
Extending to the furthest sight

We are Lightworkers
Calling forth into the
Depths with forgiveness,
Extending the eternity of
God's grace to all we meet.

We, the workers of light declare
Infinite Gratitude as our reality
Made manifest.

We, the workers of light
Are the illumination of unity
In the night of duality

We are Lightworkers
Dedicated to the highest truth
Committed to the broadest love
Devoted to the deepest faith
Extending to the furthest sight

We are Lightworkers,
Eternal adventurers, surfing
The waves of sublime peace,
Carving the ripples echoing
Eternally.

We, the workers of light declare
The Infinite River as our reality
Sourced.

We, the workers of light
Are the illumination of unity
In the night of duality

We are Lightworkers
Dedicated to highest truth
Committed to broadest love
Devoted to deepest faith
Extending to furthest sight

We are Lightworkers,
We declare this NOW.

(11/21/2007 1:53am)

Part 2

~ a journey with love ~

...let us walk with love, shall we?

~statement of principle~

True Self does reveal the path
of the will to the Kingdom Within.

Love runs through the universal soul
to all who choose conditionless joy.

Duty demands the choice of
self-purification for the materialization
of humanity's true imagination.

Relaxed focus and intentive thought
are the conduits of the empowered
trinity above.

The cycle of lives completes
with the realization that I must
be sacrificed for the greater.

(2/20/2006 7:30 pm)

~ blessings of luv ~

forgiveness *Is*,

for Forgiveness *Lives* in Light,
in The Place where Giving is...

and in That Place there lives Grace...

a soothing touch,
a sacred smile,
a heart's embrace,

for in the Sacred Heart of Love
is The Place where Glowing is...

and in That Place is the function of How...

in happiness Now,
in gratitude Now,
in love Now,

because within This Place,

This Place of Grace,

is the Living Place beyond time-and-space...

and did you know

this place of Love
is sent on the wings of a Dove

through peace and purity,
and blessings of love

so ~ see ~ here and now

~ breathe ~ here and now……

<inhale>…
<yawn while exhaling>…

aaaaaahhhhhhhhhhhhhhhhhhhhhhh

and be here and now :)

~ peace through you ~

(11/2008)

~ Love Breathes In All Ways Always ~

An amazing experience ain't it?

to be fully liberated from constraints so ingrained...
to be expressed in ways never thought possible...

and the energy Rises!

What a Bliss to know and receive
an unconditional well spring of ecstasy...
what to do with all this Blessing of Glee?
How 'bout give to every living flee, or knat,
or rat, or bat, or cat, or dog, or horse, or, or,
hey, why not give it to everything.

Fully expressed...from all the way "down stairs"
to all the way "up"...

and the energy Rises!

Blissing, buzzing, breathing, panting...
letting the energy RISE...

No specific need to be in a physical action...
Just letting the energy RISE...

Breathe it into the Heart...
Guide the motions of it like an Art...

From the One Soul in Me to the One Soul in You...
Liberating your energy...
Liberating your heart...
Knowing your divinity...
Realizing Your Part...

Being Free to Love, IN ALL WAYS...

and the energy Rises!

Not needing specific actions,
just extending the heart.

And as two become One in You,
the "male" aspect merges with the "female"...

The Mother converges with the Father...
The Love unites with the Light...

This here unification is the Sexuality of Life...

The genetically coded body;
an instrument of communication...

Deep Inside;
The Spirit that Communicates.

The Spirit is the Source,
The Source is the Life...

To KNOW the Freedom of Love and Light;
UNIFIED into Endless Sight.

no One that You meet is any different in Light,
it is All the One...

Giving it to All is Receiving it from All
All is One,
One is All...

The sight of the encasing flesh,
merely a perception in light...
& still, deep down (& up), there is the Light.

RISING
BLISSING
BUZZING
RADIATING

Being Free in the expression of Light,
Being Free in the giving of Love.

And Remembering there need be no
specific outward sign...

It All Rises In Energy

~ Loving You Always in ALL WAYS ~

(11/2008)

~ Love Rising ~

Sun is shining… even at night.

Flowers emerge from a seed.. even buried in shit.

Expansion occurs Now… even if you think it
doesn't.

.

.

.

then silence sets in

.

.

.

then more silence

.

.

.

and as if through a fog
a child within wakes to
find a flower on the heart
where shit used to be,
and the sun shining
in the mind where night
was found,

.

.

.

then more silence

.

.

.

and still more silence

.

.

.

and in a moments time,
right before the eyes
the world morphs into
the playground
of Heaven
in which
all expansion everywhere
just happens to be
fully illuminated
Right Now.

~ LOVE IS RISING ~

(11/2008)

~ of love, for love, by love, to love ~

they swim, and fly, and walk, and swing, and dance,
and twist and turn…

these sweet sweet melodies…
dancing in the legs,
singing in the arms
and loving in the heart…

the passage of time
don' really mean any-thing,
it can only bring more
sweet sweet melodies

the harmonies of Life
living Life into Life…

the serendipity of Breath,
breathing Breath into Breath…

the synchronicity of Your Soul
shining Your Breath of Life
~

~

~

and sometimes forgetting Life,
but never living without it…

so often in learning,
when we must only remember…

remembering to smile,
remembering to laugh,
and remembering to love…

if for no other reason than

to smile,
to laugh,
to love…

Freedom Lives…
and it must be living for it to Live

so get on with living
for it never ends…
~

~

~

in these sweet sweet melodies,
smiling with these sweet sweet melodies,
laughing in these sweet sweet melodies
loving in these sweet sweet melodies
~

~

~

hahahahahahah aaaaahhhhhhhhhahaha
~

~

~

< inhaling……………………………>
< swallowing >
< exhaling……………………………>
~

~

~

(12/2008)

~ love in between ~

as the heart opens
so too does love grow…

and as the love flows,
so too does the opening grow…

and then, as if by miracle,
the love becomes the ~eye~…

and as the love vibes,
so too does Life thrive…

holding the value of love as pure,
creates love between the pair…

for when the love is given,
so too is it received…

and in the receiving is the giving,
and the giving is the receiving,
so, in essence, it is all the same…

Love given is Love received,
and as Love is received,
so too is ~ more ~ Love given…

and onward to infinity,

exponentially,

ever-existingly,

for love knows no boundaries,
as in – no time and no space…

for love,
being the ever-present essence
of this moment's ever-so Present Exuberance...

living in the Effulgence,
of this ever-present blesson...

the lesson is the blessin
and the blessin is the lesson...

never failing to ~ see ~ the wisdom,
the wisdom of the Sun,
shining ever-pre~SUN~tly...

as if the Sun of Creation is
the living Heart of Imagination...

Creativity without explanation,
and Humbly in exaltation,
as the Sun of the Creating One...

The One Creating the Sun,
The Sun expressing the Life...

The Life Giving ever-present One,
Like the presence of the Sun,
in the Heart of the Living One...

if I am Aware of my Living in some way,
the I Am Aware of my Living,
and as consequence, I Am the Living One...

As is the ~ essence ~ of every Living thing,
the One in awareness,
the One beyond appearances...

beyond the perceivably appearing reality,

in the dimension of Spirit,
the depth of the Living One,
the height of the Rising One,
the width of the Expanding One,
the presence of the Giving One...

never faking on giving some,
as the giving some is the getting some...

no selfishness here,
only condition-less-ly blessing...

Living in the Ever-Present blesson,
that is Life's most holy extension...

knowing only Honoring in Connection,
and giving Honor in Connection...

the connection in Awareness
is in the awareness of the Connecting One...

The ever-living One...

ever-Living One,

Ever living...

ever

living
~
~~
~~~
~~~~
~~~~~
~~~~~~
~~~~~~

~~~~~
~~~
~~
~

the
ever
living
ONE
the
ever
living
ONE
the
ever
living
ONE

~
~~
~~~
~~~~
~~~~~
~~~~~~
~~~~~
~~~~
~~~
~~
~

as in the
One In This
Instance of existence
Forwarding
the Love
onto
every
Living
One
forwarding

this
on
through
the Heart
of the
One,

the
One
In You

(12/2008)

~ falling while flying ~

there is no depth
to this love

I Am forever falling

there is no height
to this love

I Am forever flying

into
through
with
by &
for

this Love

I Am forever falling

no need to quantify,
it is infinite

no need to direct,
it is everywhere

I Am forever flying

into now
through now
with now
by now &
for now

I Am this Love…

into you
through you
with you
by you &
for you

I Am forever falling

the width is eternally
without boundary

the length is eternally
with non-boundary

I Am forever flying

and as the waves
of grace radiate;

these ripples echo,
and eternity lives

as I fall
&
as I fly

I merge in you
and flow through you
being one with you,
& by Your loving,

I Am Free

for You...

(12/2008)

~ without word ~

Light knows,
Love flows,
Life goes…

Insight shows,
Breath rows,
Spirit sows,

Forever free,
Forever free,
Forever free,

Give to Me
Give to Ye
Give to We…

What is there to say when all is being said?

What is there to do when all is being done?

What is there to be when all is being?

A time not found is a time un-bound…

A space without bound is a space forever sound…

Free in Light through Love in Life……………

(02/2009)

~ Knowing ~

What do you want to know that you do not already Know?

What can you know other than what you see?

What can you see other than what you choose to believe?

What can you believe other than what you perceive?

As a sense arises, a perception follows...

As an awareness observes, a sense arises...

As a presence is, an awareness observes...

As Life lives, a presence is...

There within Life must Knowing be found if one should ever desire to un-confound...

There within Grace must desire be placed if one should ever wish to escape...

There within...

There within...

There within...

(02/2009)

~ Feeling ~

Navigating the ethers with an empty mind,

Operating the consciousness with an open heart,

Living the soul with a recognized essence...

Purified in the fires of honesty,

Distilled in the boiler of transparency,

Crystallized in the core of perpetuity...

Release...

Emptying the mind and embracing the presence,

Opening the heart and flowing the essence,

Recognizing essence and creating...

Reveal...

(02/2009)

~ Being ~

Restitution has been paid,

Life is returned to its rightful owner,

The One-Love Living…

Resonance is resounding,

Redemption has been received,

Atonement has been delivered,

Every Living One…

Re-cognition is realizing,

Revelation has been revealed,

Divine *Will* is disclosed to its revealer,

The In-Light-Full One…

(02/2009)_

~ on the flip side ~

With love, love is Known.
without love, love is unknown.

Forever must we Be
with love
if ever we want to Be
with love.

Forever are we Free
with love
and ever will we BE
with love.

And on the flip side…

Without love is without life,
without life is with death,
with death is the illusion of sight,
the illusion of sight is seeing no light.

Seeing no light is
eternal damnation;
ever are we damned
if we deny revelation.

And on the flip side…

Revelation reveals the revealing,
revealing reality into realization;
Whereas,
Deceiving deceives the deceiver,
whom deceives only the deceiver.

~ freshness of essence ~

a spring breeze,
a cool summer's night;
an autumn sunrise,
a white winter morn…

flowing with essence
fresh in the moment,
free in the sea
of ever-living eternity…

the fragrance of a flower,
the brilliance of a sunset;
the beaming of a rainbow,
the whisking of the wind…

coursing,
originating,
liberating,
creating…

upon the mountain top,
below in the value hollow,
all across the sea,
into every living thing…

while blessing
and remembering
in presence,
and essence,

life
lives
forever
fresh

~ Love ~

Many words are known to
communicate meaning, and
yet, the only meaning is a
Truth that gives rise to the
reality of communication.

For a soul wandering through
the ethers of eternity,
wondering who, what, when,
where and how this Truth
comes to Be;

Perhaps an embrace of Life's
saving grace that permeates
all of time and space and
stares us straight in the face is
the One with the answer.

Never will we be known if
we seek not to become
Known, and forever will we
feel the pangs of suffering
until we re-cognize the reality
of who we are Being.

Being need not be a concept,
for Being already is. If Being
were not, we would BE not.
And yet, here we are, Being,
not within a thought
contained in the frame of
time and space, but beyond
the horizon of a dual night
and day.

Relative is as relative does,
and beyond the absolutely
relative, is a reality not so
relative.

Absolute is as absolute does,
and into this un-nameable
place is that which is beyond
all relative time-and-space.

There is no up and there is no
down; no left and no right; no
in, no out; no forward, no
backward.

And as the knowledge of the
dual natured fruit picked
from the tree of good and evil
leaves the mind, the infinite
vastness of the absolute is
again cognized.

And as the cognition of light
eternal and love ever-lasting
permeates the mind and
heart; the floodgates of
freedom are released, and the
life-giving waters carry the
raft of our soul through the
sea of eternity, into the land
flowing with milk and honey.

And on earth, heaven comes
to be seen. Not in some far
off future, or in some life after
death adventure, but in

the living presence of life
permeating the entirety of the
cosmos and beyond.

In a word – Love. For Love,
there is no boundary, it
moves, lives and breathes life
into everything; absolutely
everything.

For in the essence of
everything is the living,
breathing presence of the One
sustaining Love permeating
the entirety of existence
existing as this cosmic
blesson.

The nature of Nature begets
the perception, and in the
nature of life-essence, the
perception is light-presence.

And when the light shines,
the mind of time comes to be
released into thee Mind of
non-time, a present-tense
awareness knowing only the
jubilant exuberance of this
most holy effulgence.

Through the effulgent
radiance of life living in this
most holy instance, the
vibration of love moving
through the heart increases
the libations of life-giving

waters that carry the soul
through the eternal ethers
of this cosmic sea of living
essence.

Only One Present-tense
Essence; only knowing
Supreme Freshness.

Hence the One sense, the
ever-living tense; a verse of
science illuminating the
intellect beyond the neglect
of ignorance.

Thence a radiance, only
requiring an awareness to
embrace an itty-bitty
willingness to open the center
chest freshness liberated
through forgiveness.

Whence illumination
enlightens, and forgiveness
brightens, a soul wandering
through the ethers of eternity,
wondering who, what when,
where, and how this Truth
comes to Be, this Being is no
longer confounded in the
unfounded identity of past-
tense ignorance nor future-
tense hesitance.

Operating in the mode of
consistent vigilance of Life's
One Love Essence

And in this, the many words
used to communicate usher
forth in a flow of poetic
songs that sing praises in
exaltation of the dance of
Truth, also known as the
happy-dance.

Operating happiness brings
smiles & laughter through
which the all-pervasive
presence flows; and the
energy increases as the love
rises; for in Truth, energy and
love are no different, the
same One Love Essence of
the present-tense instance.

And in the wandering and
wondering of who, what,
when, where, & how of Truth
Being, perhaps the embrace
of love's saving grace
permeating all time & space
bestows the wisdom of this
blesson, the One Love lesson
that is forever blessing all of
existence in this most holy
instant; the present-tense
essence...

P E A C E................

Of The First Magnitude

~I~

~Volume 1~
Facing Revelation
An Emerging

~Volume 2~
iRise
An Algorhythm of Freedom

~Volume 3~
Quantum Engineering
Introspecting the Rabbit Hole

~Volume 4~
Algorhythmic Insight
Poetic Analysis of the Journey

More From Michael Phoenix

- On Eros
  - Cōnsēnsiō, vol. 1
  - Sēnsuālitās, vol. 2
  - Sublīmātiō, vol. 3
- Of the First Magnitude
  - Facing Revelation: An Emerging, vol. 1
  - iRise: An Algorhythm of Freedom, vol. 2
  - Quantum Engineering: Introspecting the Rabbit Hole, vol. 3
- Body Integration & the One Minute Workout: Learning to Love the Body You're In

www.ingramcontent.com/pod-product-compliance
Lightning Source LLC
Chambersburg PA
CBHW031700040426
42452CB00028B/788